ROCK 'N' ROLL

AND OTHER DANCE CRAZES

RITA STOREY

SEA-TO-SEA
Mankato Collingwood London

ROCK 'N' ROLL

AND OTHER DANCE CRAZES

Rock and roll (also called rock 'n' roll) was born in the 1950s. It was a brand new style of music, dance, and fashion that teenagers made their own. Many parents disapproved of it. But soon the dance craze swept around the world—to be followed by many others.

Dance crazes are not a modern thing. But the speed with which they spread has increased. The invention of the record player and records helped dance crazes catch on across countries and continents, especially when records became smaller, lighter, and cheaper. In 1954, the first transistor radios went on sale, making it possible to listen to popular music channels at any time. When television became widely available, crazes of music and dance could go global practically overnight.

Why should *I* dance?

Dancing is good for everyone. It's a great way to get in shape. All types of dancing are a form of aerobic exercise, which encourages your heart and lungs to work hard. Over time, this will help them to become stronger and get *you* in better condition.

The food we eat provides our body with the energy it needs to work properly. But if we eat more calories than our body needs, these are stored as fat. Dancing makes your body burn off calories. Your muscles will strengthen and become firmer, and your body will become more toned.

Dancing makes you happy

When you exercise, your brain makes a hormone called seratonin, which makes you feel happy. So if you're feeling miserable, put down the chocolate, put on the music, and get dancing.

There are so many types of dance there really is something for everyone. You can do the dance moves in this book on your own or with a friend, and work at a pace that suits you.

Dancing can even boost your brain power. Putting together dance steps increases your coordination and helps keep your mind alert.

Last but not least, dancing is fun. So what are you waiting for? Turn up the music and get moving!

Contents

Let's get moving

Why do I have to warm up?

Before you learn any new dance steps and begin to put them together, it is important to warm up your muscles so you don't get a cramp or strain a muscle. You may only be able to do the exercises a couple of times to start with, but don't give up. Just do a few more repeats each time. A warmup should last about ten minutes.

There are warmup moves in each of the four books in the *Get Dancing* series. You can combine them to make a routine.

Aerobic exercises

The first set of exercises is aerobic, which means it improves your breathing and circulation. Aerobic exercise increases your oxygen intake by making your heart beat faster. To do it, you have to keep on the move all the time. Each set of aerobic exercises is designed to be repeated. If you are not used to exercise and feel your pulse starting to race, stop and jog on the spot to keep warm.

AEROBIC EXERCISE
TWIST

1 Face forward with your feet together, your heels slightly off the ground, and your knees bent. Hold your elbows bent at just under shoulder height.

2 With a little jump, twist your waist, hips, and feet to the left, and swing your right arm out to the right. Keep your left arm bent in front of you.

3 With a little jump, twist your waist, hips, and feet to the right, and swing your left arm out to the left. Bend your right arm in front of you.

Repeat 10 times to the left, and 10 times to the right.

4

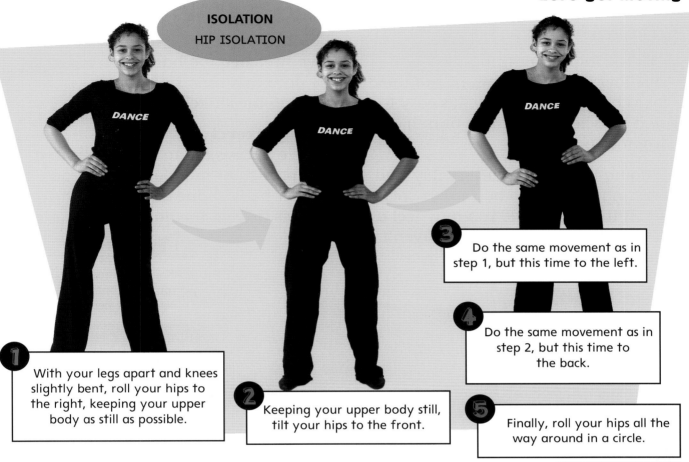

ISOLATION
HIP ISOLATION

1 With your legs apart and knees slightly bent, roll your hips to the right, keeping your upper body as still as possible.

2 Keeping your upper body still, tilt your hips to the front.

3 Do the same movement as in step 1, but this time to the left.

4 Do the same movement as in step 2, but this time to the back.

5 Finally, roll your hips all the way around in a circle.

Repeat twice.

Body isolations

The second set of exercises is a body isolation. This type of exercise teaches you to move parts of your body individually, which is important for rock and roll dancing.

What to wear

Wear something comfortable to do a warmup, such as loose-fitting leggings (not jeans), a T-shirt, and a loose, long-sleeved top you can take off when you have warmed up.

You can do the routine in bare feet, sneakers, or jazz shoes. Don't do it in socks, or you may slip.

Dance to the music

You will need at least two pieces of music for the warmup. The first is for the aerobic exercises. It should be energetic and upbeat, to make everyone feel enthusiastic. It can also be used for body isolations, which are sharp, quick moves.

The second piece of music will be used for the stretches and toning exercises (see page 6). Gentle, relaxing music is best for this part of the warmup.

Let's get moving

Stretches

The most important thing to remember about stretches is that they should be done gradually. It's easy to pull a muscle by pushing yourself too hard, too soon.

Try doing the exercises every day and stretching just a little bit further each time. If it hurts, STOP. You may feel a little stiff the next day if you haven't been exercising regularly, but you shouldn't be in pain. If you are, you have stretched too hard. Stop for a few days and then start slowly building the stretches up again.

Toning exercises

These exercises are to strengthen and tone particular muscles, giving you a better body shape and strong muscles to hold the dance moves.

STRETCH AND TONE
LEG STRETCH

1 Stand with your feet apart and parallel to each other. Put your right hand behind your back. Keeping your back flat, bend at the waist and stretch forward with your left hand as far as you can.

2 Reach down to touch your right foot with both hands. Relax your head.

3 Reach down to touch the floor between your feet with both hands.

4 Do the same move as step 1 but this time with your *left* hand behind your back, and stretching forward with your *right* hand. Do the same move as step 2, but this time reach down to touch your *left* foot with both hands. Repeat step 3.

Repeat twice.

Cool it!

At the end of a dance session, it is important to do a cool-down routine to help prevent stiffness the next day. The routine concentrates on stretching exercises that stretch out and relax the muscles. To be effective, each stretch should be held for a slow count of ten. A cool-down routine should last for five to ten minutes.

Each of the four books in the *Get Dancing* series contains cool-down stretches. You can use a combination from different books if you wish.

Hold each move for a slow count of 10.

COOL IT! 1
ARM STRETCH

1 Intertwine your fingers behind your body and stretch your arms as far back and up as they will go. (Do not arch your back.)

COOL IT! 2
HAMSTRING STRETCH

1 With your feet together and your toes pointing forward, step back on your left foot and lower your bottom down as far as you can. Keep your back flat. Repeat with the right foot.

COOL IT! 3
UPPER ARM STRETCH

1 Intertwine your fingers in front of your body, with your palms facing away from you. Stretch your arms forward as far as they will go. To increase the stretch, drop your head between your arms.

Rock 'n' roll dancing

Rock 'n' roll is danced with a partner. It is a faster, more athletic version of a dance called the jive. The jive steps are shown on pages 8–11.

Music for jive and rock and roll has four beats to the bar (see glossary). But if you danced each move to one beat of the music, you would be going too fast. So it is danced "off beat"—the moves are "one *and* two *and* three *and* four." You move from one position to another on the "*and*" counts.

Put on some music and practice the jive to get used to it. As you do so, bend your knees slightly and swing your hips to the beat of the music.

JIVE
(FOUR BASIC STEPS)

1 Girl's left arm to the boy's right shoulder. Boy's left arm to the girl's right shoulder. Still holding hands, swing your arms down and then up to position 2.
(Don't worry too much about your feet: the movement will start to come naturally as you dance the steps.)

2 Girl's right arm to the boy's left shoulder. Boy's right arm to the girl's left shoulder. Still holding hands, swing your arms down and then up to position 3.

Dance to the music

Bill Haley and the Comets: "See You Later Alligator," "Shake, Rattle and Roll," "Rock Around the Clock." Elvis Presley: "Jailhouse Rock." Little Richard: "Tutti Frutti," "Good Golly, Miss Molly." Chuck Berry: "Sweet Little Sixteen," "Roll Over Beethoven." Jerry Lee Lewis: "Great Balls of Fire," "Whole Lot of Shaking Going On." Danny and the Juniors: "At the Hop." Queen: "Crazy Little Thing Called Love."

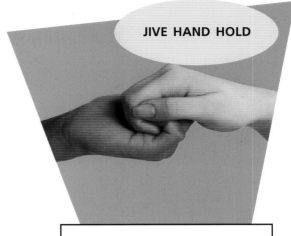

JIVE HAND HOLD

The boy grips the girl's hands from underneath.

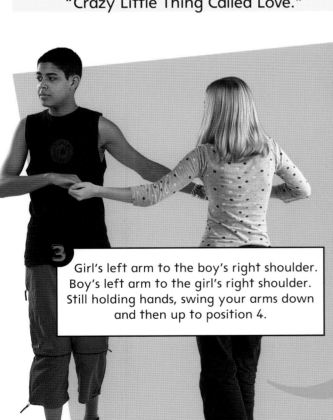

3 Girl's left arm to the boy's right shoulder. Boy's left arm to the girl's right shoulder. Still holding hands, swing your arms down and then up to position 4.

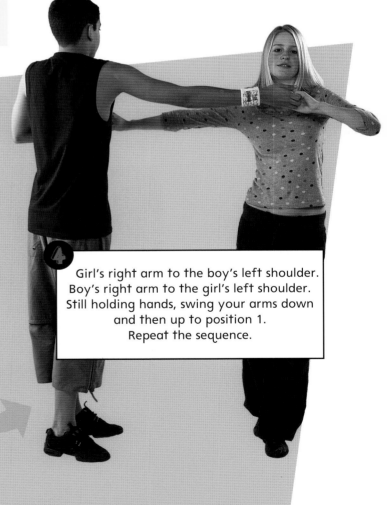

4 Girl's right arm to the boy's left shoulder. Boy's right arm to the girl's left shoulder. Still holding hands, swing your arms down and then up to position 1. Repeat the sequence.

Rock 'n' roll dancing

TURN AND BACK STEP

1 2 3 Perform moves 1 to 3 of the basic jive steps on pages 8 and 9.

5 The girl turns counterclockwise under the boy's arm.

4 The boy holds his right hand up to start the turn. He lets go of the girl's right hand.

6 The girl continues to turn until facing slightly to the right.

7 The girl turns back the other way.

8 End the turn with both boy and girl back in position 1.

ROCK AROUND THE CLOCK

Rock 'n' roll was a dance craze that hit the U.S. in the 1950s. It was based on many of the dance styles that were popular in the 1940s, such as the jitterbug, the jive, and the lindy hop.

Rock 'n' roll was the first style of music and fashion that teenagers seized for themselves.

Teenagers arrive

Before 1950, there was no such thing as a teenager! Young people of 13–19 were treated either as children, or as younger versions of their parents. But in the 1950s, young people had more freedom, independence, and money to spend than their parents' generation. They did not want the music and clothes of their parents; they wanted to be different. Soon, young people in this age group came to be called "teenagers."

Rock 'n' roll music had a new energy and a rebellious image, and teenagers loved it. The dance created to go with it was athletic and exhilarating.

The coffee bar scene

Coffee bars with jukeboxes were opened all over the North America. They were popular with teenagers, who gathered there to hear the new songs before going out to buy them.

You can rent rock 'n' roll outfits for boys and girls from costume suppliers.

TV for teenagers

American Bandstand, a music show on television aimed at teenagers, showed young people dancing to the new rock 'n' roll records. It set trends in both music and fashion.

Movies about teenagers, such as *Blackboard Jungle*, attracted big audiences. This movie featured the song "Rock Around the Clock," by Bill Haley and the Comets, as its theme tune.

Rock 'n' roll is a quicker and jerkier form of the jive, with a shorter arm movement, and additional steps. Instead of moving your arm right up to your partner's shoulder, it only goes to just above waist height. This is called the close arm hold. The dance moves become quicker and closer.

What to wear

In 1950s, the main fashion looks for American teenagers were "greaser" or "preppy."

Greasers wore black leather jackets and blue jeans. Preppies were neat and tidy. Preppy girls wore circular skirts with a net petticoat. Scoop-neck blouses, turtlenecks, or shirts with three-quarter sleeves were popular. A scarf was often knotted at the side of the neck.

In Britain in the 1950s, there was a youth movement called the teddy boys, influenced by greasers and preppies. The clothes they wore were similar to the clothes worn by these dancers.

ROCK 'N' ROLL
CLOSE ARM HOLD

Rock 'n' roll danced with a close arm hold.

Rock 'n' roll dancing

In rock 'n' roll dancing, various steps can be combined with the basic moves. These include kick steps and slides. (In the 1950s, groups of boys sometimes danced kick steps and slides without partners.)

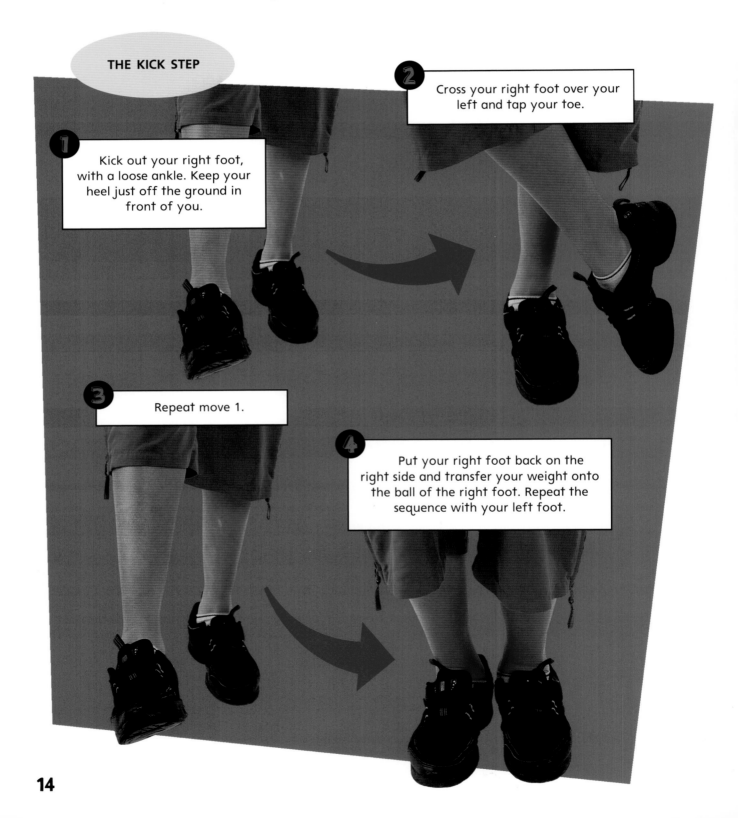

THE KICK STEP

1. Kick out your right foot, with a loose ankle. Keep your heel just off the ground in front of you.

2. Cross your right foot over your left and tap your toe.

3. Repeat move 1.

4. Put your right foot back on the right side and transfer your weight onto the ball of the right foot. Repeat the sequence with your left foot.

Do the hand jive

Rock 'n' roll is energetic and athletic, and is danced with a partner. But the hand jive can be done on your own. It is ideal for taking a breather from more strenuous dance moves. It can even be "danced" sitting down.

Prompt corner
The 1970s movie *Grease* is about teenagers in the rock and roll era of the 1950s. Watch it to get ideas for dancing and clothes.

THE HAND JIVE

1 Place the elbow of one arm on the back of the opposite hand, point your finger, and circle your hand from the wrist. Swap arms.

2 Hold your hands palms down and move them over each other in a scissor movement.

3 Make your hands into fists and tap one on top of the other. Swap hands.

The twist

The twist is probably the easiest dance ever to have become a craze. Maybe it became so popular because everybody could do it! The twist craze started in the early 1960s and lasted until the mid-1960s.

What to wear

In the early 1960s, straight, knee-length skirts, matching pullovers and cardiagans, and fitted dresses were popular for young women. Young men wore suits with narrow slacks. By the mid-1960s, miniskirts and pop art dresses were fashionable. Young men began to grow their hair longer and wear more colorful clothes.

THE TWIST

1 Stand with one foot slightly in front of the other, with your front knee bent.

2 Swivel your front foot from side to side. Swing your hips and move your arms in the opposite direction as if you were drying off your back with a towel.

TWISTING THE NIGHT AWAY

Chubby Checker had a hit with his song "The Twist" in 1960 and performed it on *American Bandstand*. The twist became a worldwide dance craze.

The twist was the first dance that could be done completely alone.

A very easy dance

Because it was danced more or less on one spot, the dance took up very little room and so was ideal for dancing in crowds. There were no complicated steps to remember. The only variation on the theme was twisting down as low as you could and back up again.

The twist was followed by lots of other dance crazes, such as the pony, the swim, and the locomotion.

Dance to the music

Chubby Checker: "The Twist," "Let's Twist Again." The Isley Brothers: "Twist and Shout" (also sung by the Beatles). Sam Cooke: "Twisting the Night Away."

Chubby Checker and his partner doing the twist.

Disco dancing

Disco was a music and dance craze of the 1970s. One major dance to come from the discos was the hustle. It was danced with a partner, but each couple would make up their own version, often breaking away from each other to dance individual moves. The moves here can be added to the hustle (pages 20–21).

DISCO MOVE 1

1 Bend your knees and point across your body and down at the floor with your right hand.

2 Punch your right hand up into the air. Straighten your front leg.

DISCO MOVE 2

1 Roll your arms forward and lean forward.

2 Roll your arms backward and lean back.

DISCO FEVER

What to wear

In the 1970s, people who went to discos "dressed to impress." The fashions were all about glamor, glitter, sparkle, sequins, and frills: anything that would get you noticed when you danced.

Discos often used ultraviolet lights, which made white clothes glow in the semidarkness. Dressing in white was very popular for this reason.

Hotpants were all the rage for girls in the early 1970s. Later on, clingy, all-in-one "jumpsuits" were worn by both sexes.

Fabric with metalic threads running through it (Lurex) was also fashionable, as were gold and silver clothes and accessories.

Platform shoes were a fashion essential for both men and women. The platform under the sole was often at least 2 inches (5 cm) high with a 5-inch (12-cm) chunky heel, but some people wore platforms that were up to 6 inches (15 cm) high.

The word "discothèque" or "disco" is French. It is a play on the word "bibliothèque," which means "library." The word was invented to name a French nightclub. The idea was that the new club would have a library of records instead of books. In 1977, a hugely popular movie called *Saturday Night Fever* was released. It starred John Travolta and Karen Lyn Gorney and told the story of a young man who was crazy about disco dancing. Much of the music was by the Bee Gees. The movie caused an explosion in the number of dance schools teaching disco, in particular the hustle.

Pile on the glitter and sparkle. You can go totally wild with disco gear!

Disco dancing

THE HUSTLE

1 Stand facing each other, holding hands.

2 Let go of one hand and step out to the side with your free arm held up.

3 The boy then turns inward, putting his free arm behind the girl's back and taking hold of her free hand.

Dance to the music

The Bee Gees: "Stayin' Alive." Van McCoy: "The Hustle." The Village People: "YMCA." Artists such as KC and the Sunshine Band, Kool and the Gang, Donna Summer, and Gloria Gaynor..

20

You then walk around in a circle. To give this dance the right feel, don't just walk—strut!

Let go of one hand and step out to the side with your free arm held up.

Go back to step 1.

Disco dancing

MORE DISCO MOVES

DISCO MOVE 3
CHICKEN WINGS

1 Bend your elbows and flap your "wings" like a chicken.

DISCO MOVE 4
TURN AND CLAP

1 Turn counterclockwise, through a complete turn, and then clap.

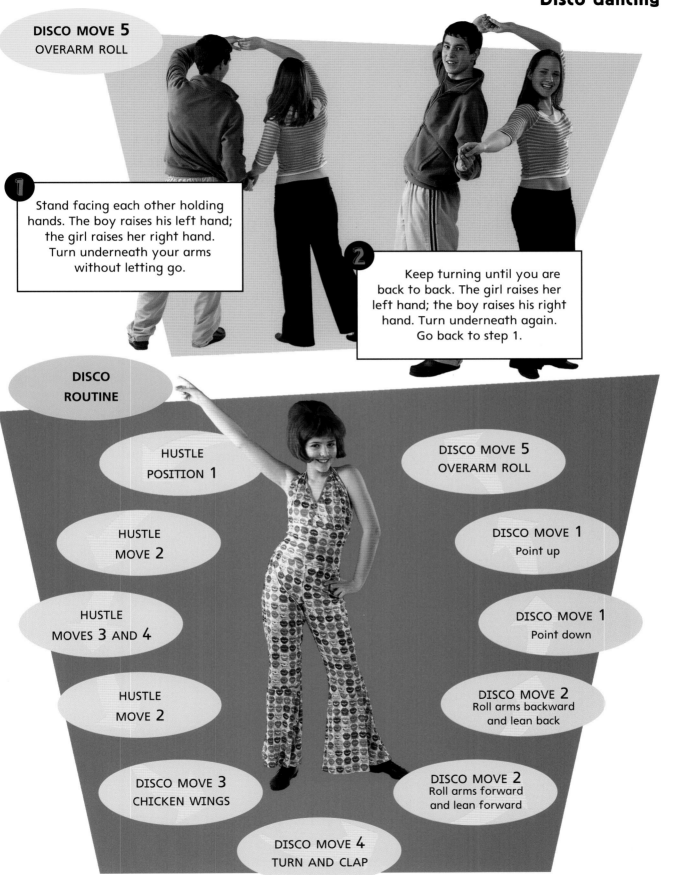

DISCO MOVE 5
OVERARM ROLL

1 Stand facing each other holding hands. The boy raises his left hand; the girl raises her right hand. Turn underneath your arms without letting go.

2 Keep turning until you are back to back. The girl raises her left hand; the boy raises his right hand. Turn underneath again. Go back to step 1.

DISCO ROUTINE

HUSTLE POSITION 1

HUSTLE MOVE 2

HUSTLE MOVES 3 AND 4

HUSTLE MOVE 2

DISCO MOVE 3 CHICKEN WINGS

DISCO MOVE 4 TURN AND CLAP

DISCO MOVE 5 OVERARM ROLL

DISCO MOVE 1 Point up

DISCO MOVE 1 Point down

DISCO MOVE 2 Roll arms backward and lean back

DISCO MOVE 2 Roll arms forward and lean forward

The salsa

In salsa dancing, the top half of your body remains fairly still. The characteristic style of the dance is created by the way your hips, legs, and arms roll, wiggle, and sway as you dance to the music.

There are four simple steps to the basic dance, which use four beats of music. When you have learned them, add the hip, leg, and arm movements.

The four steps consist of making a step on three beats of the music, and tapping your foot on the fourth. These basic steps can be done sideways, backward, and forward. Pages 24, 26, and 27 give you a taste of salsa, with three types of basic salsa step.

Salsa is danced with a partner, and other more complicated steps are added to the basic moves.

BASIC SALSA STEPS
TO THE SIDE

1 Step out with your left foot, and transfer your weight to your left leg.

2 Step together. Transfer your weight to your right leg.

3 Step out with your left foot, and transfer your weight to your left leg.

4 With your weight on your left leg, tap your right foot alongside your left foot. Do the same moves, this time going in the opposite direction.

LATIN AMERICAN RHYTHMS

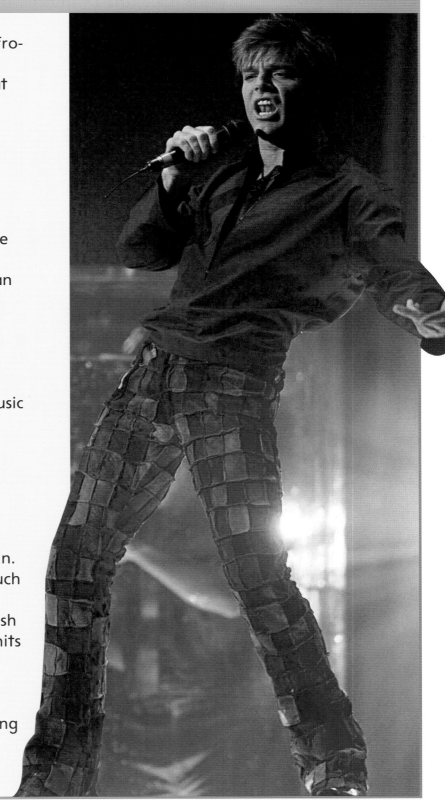

Salsa music is a mixture of Afro-Caribbean and Latin-Cuban music. The style of dance that goes with it combines moves from all the major Cuban dances such as the rumba, mambo, and cha-cha-cha.

Tasty music

In the 1970s, rock music was very popular and people were not very interested in Latin dance music. A small American record company called Fania Records wanted to attract people to Latin dance music again. So they gave it a new name, "salsa," meaning "sauce," to show that the music was tasty! Their idea was successful, and created a new interest in Latin American music.

Salsa crazy!

In the 1980s and 1990s, salsa became popular all over again. Latin American music stars such as Gloria Estefan and Ricky Martin (right), and the Spanish singer Enrique Iglesias, had hits all over the world. They brought a new energy and popularity to salsa dancing. The number of people learning to salsa has soared.

The salsa

Once you feel you know the basic salsa steps, dance them with the extra hip, leg, and arm movements. Keeping your arms at waist height, move them to the rhythm of the music. At the same time, roll your hips as you transfer your weight from one leg to another.

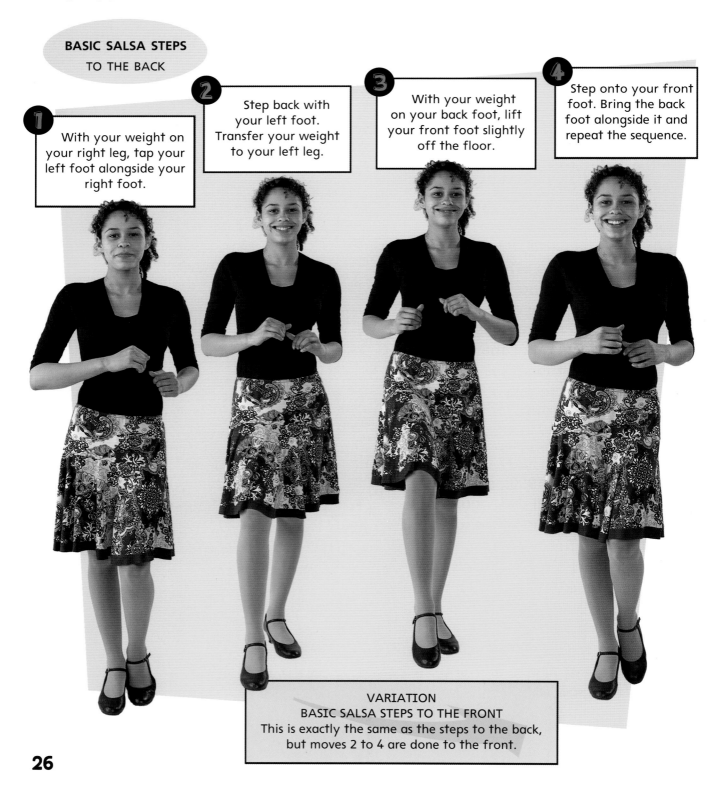

BASIC SALSA STEPS
TO THE BACK

1 With your weight on your right leg, tap your left foot alongside your right foot.

2 Step back with your left foot. Transfer your weight to your left leg.

3 With your weight on your back foot, lift your front foot slightly off the floor.

4 Step onto your front foot. Bring the back foot alongside it and repeat the sequence.

VARIATION
BASIC SALSA STEPS TO THE FRONT
This is exactly the same as the steps to the back, but moves 2 to 4 are done to the front.

Dance to the music

Gloria Estefan is one of the most popular singers of modern Latin American salsa music. She has created a style that is a blend of salsa and disco.

"Mi Tierra" (My Homeland) and "Alma Caribeña" (Caribbean Soul) are recorded in Spanish.

"Unwrapped" and "Destiny" are sung mainly in English, but still have a salsa feel.

What to wear

Girls who dance salsa tend to wear very feminine clothes, such as short, full skirts or dresses. Because salsa music stems from the countries of the Caribbean and Latin America, the clothes are usually very bright and colorful. Boys often wear bright shirts and stylish slacks.

Shoes with a smooth sole are best, because they allow you to glide across the floor.

When dancing energetic salsa with lots of different steps, girls with long hair often wear it up so it does not flick into their partner's face.

BASIC SALSA
PARTNER STEP

1 Face your partner and hold hands. Step to one side.

2 Step your feet together.

3 Step out from your partner. Bring the foot in again and tap.

Other dance crazes

There have been dance crazes throughout the history of dance. Some of the dances that are well established today started out as dance crazes.

For example, the waltz was a dance craze that came from Germany. It was considered highly unsuitable at first, because dancing couples had to hold each other in a close embrace. (At this time, all dances with partners were done holding hands at arm's length.)

The charleston
In the 1920s, a craze for dancing the charleston swept through North America and the UK. It was seen in dance halls, on the stage, and in early movies. The dance was popular

Dance the charleston as a 1920s flapper.

with both boys and girls. Girls who danced it were known as "flappers."

Animal dances
A whole "zoo" of animal dances came after the charleston: the bunny hug, the grizzly bear, the chicken scratch, and many more. These were danced to ragtime music. Dancers mimicked the movement of the animals. The most famous animal dance was the turkey trot. In this dance, a man would trot toward his partner flapping his arms like a turkey, while his partner did the same going backward. This dance was considered so outrageous that it was banned by the Pope!

The lindy hop
The next important dance craze to hit North America and Europe was the lindy hop. It was created to be danced to the new rhythm of swing jazz. The lindy hop first appeared at the Savoy Ballroom, in

Harlem in the 1920s. The lindy hop introduced the air-step to dancing. This was when a man swung his partner up into the air. The lindy hop, the jitterbug (a version of the lindy hop), and the jive went on to become rock 'n' roll.

Dance crazes of the 1960s

The arrival of the twist seemed to open the floodgates for hundreds of different dance styles. The watusi, the hitchhiker, the shake, the swim, the locomotion, and the stroll were just a few of them. Most were devised to be danced to just one record and then disappeared without a trace. None of them lasted in the same way as the twist.

Disco crazes

In the 1970s, disco dancers invented their own collection of dance crazes. As well as the hustle (see pages 20–21) there was the freak, the bump, and also the moves associated with a hit song by the Village People, called "YMCA."

Dancing the swim involves miming the crawl, and pretending to hold your nose and bob down under the water.

Dances of the late twentieth century

At the end of the 1990s, a new craze for a type of country and western dancing called line dancing started in the U.S. It became extremely popular as country music crossed over into the mainstream music charts.

Further information

Websites

www.sixtiescity.com
Click on "Youth culture," then click on "Dance crazes."
This site has lots of information about the 60s, including the steps to many of the dances that were around at the time.

www.bustamove.com
Animated figures show all the basic salsa moves and routines. You can choose from three levels: beginner, intermediate, or advanced.

www.dancetutor.com
This site gives instructions using online video, stills, and text so you can learn any style of dance, including jive and swing.

http://usabda.org
www.ndca.org
These national dance websites contain everything you need to know about dance, including listings of where to find dance lessons in your area.

www.dancevision.com
This site offers books, videos, CDs, and DVDs about every dance form you can think of.

DVDs and videos

Anyone Can Rock 'n' Roll
A video with fifteen rock 'n' roll moves, from the very basic to advanced turns and spins.

Learn to Dance Salsa
A DVD showing all the basic dance techniques for dancing salsa.

Note to parents and teachers: Every effort has been made by the Publishers to ensure these websites are suitable for children, they are of the highest educational value, and contain no inappropriate or offensive material. Because of the nature of the Internet, however, it is impossible to guarantee that the contents of these sites will not be altered. We strongly advise that Internet access is supervised by a responsible adult.

Dancing is a fun way to get in shape, but like any form of physical exercise it has an element of risk, particularly if you are unfit, overweight, or suffer from any medical conditions. It is advisable to consult a healthcare professional before beginning any exercise program.

Glossary

Aerobic exercise   Exercise that improves breathing and circulation.

Beat   The regular pulse in music.

Beats to the bar   The way that music is divided up into segments. Each bar contains the same number of beats. (See also "Off beat.")

Coordination   The ability to move different parts of the body together at the same time.

Discothèque or disco   A club where people danced to records.

Flappers   Young women in the 1920s who dressed and behaved in what was considered to be an unconventional way.

Greasers   In 1950s, greasers were youngsters from white, blue-collar backgrounds who were involved with motorcycles or cars.

Hormone   A substance produced by the body, which affects the way the body functions.

Hotpants   Tight, skimpy shorts worn by young women in the 1970s.

Hustle   A disco dance, danced with a partner, popular in the 1970s.

Isolations   A type of exercise involving moving one part of the body without moving the rest.

Jive   A dance style where you dance with a partner to swing music.

Jukebox   An automatic record player activated by inserting coins.

Jumpsuit   An all-in-one outfit with a top and pants joined together.

Off beat   Some dance moves are danced off beat, i.e. danced to any beat in a bar other than the first one.

Pop art   Objects or scenes from everyday life, depicted by commercial art techniques such as printing.

Preppies   The name for school students in 1950s. They wore neat, tidy clothing.

Rock 'n' roll   A type of popular music starting in the 1950s. It was a blend of black rhythm and blues with white country and western music.

Teddy boy   In Britain, especially during the 1950s, a tough youth wearing long narrow fitted suits and high collars.

Tone   The quality or pitch of a particular instrument or voice.

Transistor radio   A small, portable radio.

Salsa   A spicy sauce. Also a type of Latin-American dance music.

Index

This edition first published in 2007 by
Sea-to-Sea Publications
1980 Lookout Drive
North Mankato
Minnesota 56003

Copyright © Sea-to-Sea Publications 2007

Printed in China

Library of Congress Cataloging in Publication Data
Storey, Rita.
  Rock 'n' roll / by Rita Storey.
    p.cm. -- (Get dancing)
    ISBN *978-1-59771-051-0
    1. Rock and roll dancing--Juvenile literature. I.Title. II. Series.

  GV1796.R6S76 2006
  793.3'3--dc22

                            2005056766

9 8 7 6 5 4 3 2

Published by arrangement with the Watts Publishing Group Ltd., London

Series editor: Rachel Cooke
Art director: Peter Scoulding

Series designed and created for Franklin Watts by
STOREYBOOKS Ltd.

Designer: Rita Storey
Editor: Fiona Corbridge
Photography: Tudor Photography, Banbury
Dance consultants: Lucie-Grace Welsman, Joe Kelly (salsa corazon)

Picture credits
Corbis/Bettmann p.17; Corbis/Reuters p.25.

Cover images: Tudor Photography, Banbury.

All photos posed by models.
Thanks to James Boyce, Kimesha Campbell, Amba Mann, Grace
Penman, Charlie Storey, Hannah Storey, and Michael Williams.

With many thanks to Goody Two Shoes, Rugby, UK, who supplied all
the costumes.